GW00472327

Skiing Made Easy

Complete beginner to parallel turns

DAVID P MITCHELL

Copyright © 2020 David P Mitchell

All rights reserved.

ISBN-13: 979-8-65-394000-2

DEDICATION

To Ruth, Geoff, Lucy & Nathan

CONTENTS

PREFACE

This is intended as a practical guide to learning to ski, from complete beginner to parallel turns. It's based on many happy seasons of ski teaching in Val Thorens, during which time I've seen how people learn and progress - what helps and what doesn't.

I learnt to ski as an adult, and trained to be a ski instructor with BASI (the British Association of Snowsport Instructors). I've done nearly all my ski teaching at the ESF (Ecole du Ski Francais) in Val Thorens.

Why learn to ski?

The first and most important reason is because it looks (and is) great fun.

There are lots of other good reasons. It could be that it's a way to explore beautiful snow-covered mountains, or that you have a competitive spirit and you want to go faster than your brother, sister, or friend. Perhaps you'd like to be included on a work trip, or accompany a partner who is a keen skier. That's fine, as long as you also end up enjoying it.

The structure of the book

The book starts with a chapter about putting on your boots and skis, then goes through a beginner's progression from snowplough to parallel turns.

Exercises

For some of the techniques described, I suggest relevant exercises that can be used to develop and improve your skills.

Common Faults

'Common faults' sections appear once or more in each chapter. In these sections, I identify mistakes which are often made, and suggest ways of correcting them.

By the way

As well as the main content in each chapter, there's extra information under 'by the way' sub-headings. Examples include carrying your skis and using a chairlift.

The demonstrations

The skier performing most of the demonstrations in this book is Marina Michaud, who grew up in Val Thorens, and trained with the Ski Club here. She has skied competitively, and is now a ski instructor in Val Thorens; she also has a University diploma in sign language, and her ski clients include skiers who are deaf or hard of hearing.

The photos

The photos are, of course, a very important part of this book. It would be hard to follow the ideas and techniques explained, without seeing them demonstrated.

The images in this book are also presented in a photo gallery on my website and can be found at https://valthorensguide.co.uk/wp/skiing-made-easy-photo-gallery/.

Happy skiing

I hope you find this book useful, and more importantly, that you have great fun skiing and do it as often as possible.

1 PUTTING ON YOUR BOOTS & SKIS

I f you're new to skiing, the equipment you have to wear will seem foreign at first, but you'll soon get used to it.

Putting on ski boots

Whether you're buying or renting ski boots, get them from a reputable shop, to make sure that they fit well. Ill-fitting boots and painful feet are miserable.

Wear just one pair of socks. They can be thick ski/outdoor socks, or a normal pair of thin (but long) socks. Pull them up, so there are no rolls or creases in them, as anything that isn't smooth can be painful once inside ski boots.

Figure 1: pulling the tongue of the boot forward

Pull the tongue of the boot forward, and slide your foot inside. Then push the tongue back into place, making sure it goes inside the two flaps either side, not outside them.

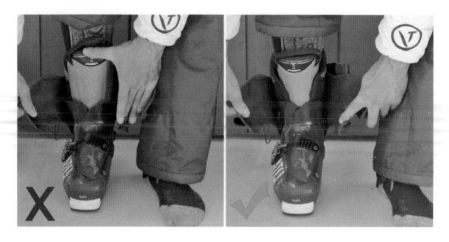

Figure 2: getting the tongue of the boot in the right position

Do up the buckles. The lower buckles, holding your foot in place, should be reasonably tight, so that when you make movements with your foot and leg, they transfer to the skis. The higher buckles, holding your shin in place, should be loose enough to allow some ankle flex, but not so loose that your shins can collapse forward.

Do up the Velcro strip at the top, known as the power strap, then put the elasticated cuff of your ski trousers over the boots.

Common faults: the elastic at the bottom of your ski trousers

The elastic at the bottom of your ski trousers goes outside the ski boot. Its purpose is to stop snow going into the boots in the unlikely (!) event of a fall.

If you make the mistake of putting the elastic inside your ski boots, after a while it will probably hurt. This might sound like a minor matter, but if you're in pain it's unlikely you'll be able to concentrate on your skiing.

It's worth mentioning that you could end up with sore shins even if you wear your equipment correctly. In that case, I recommend silicone shin protectors, which can be bought from most good ski shops, and usually solve the problem.

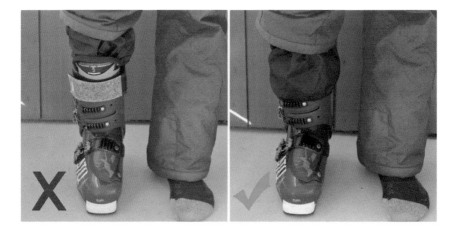

Figure 3: trouser elastic inside and outside the boot

When the elastic is safely outside your boots, you can pull the bottom of your ski trousers over it, for a professional look.

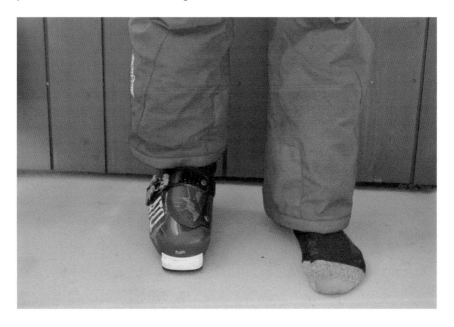

Figure 4: ski trouser leg pulled down over the boot

Putting your skis on

When you get outside onto the snow, put your skis down on level ground. Take a ski pole in each hand for balance, and stand with one foot in between your two skis, and the other lifted ready to put into your ski binding.

If you stand too far away from the ski you're trying to put on, it's hard to get your foot/boot at the right angle to go into the ski binding.

Sometimes, snow sticks to the bottom of a ski boot. This happens particularly when there's fresh, recently-fallen snow. It should be removed before putting the ski on. To do this, scrape the underneath of your boot on the front of the ski binding. Try to move your boot forwards and backwards over the binding, so as to scrape off all the snow from the whole sole.

Remember to scrape, not stamp.

Figure 5: scraping (in this case, theoretical) snow from the sole of the boot

You may see people tapping their boots with a ski pole to try to remove the snow, but that's ineffective for all but the loosest snow.

If there's stubborn hard-packed snow or ice on the sole of your boot, you might need to get a friend to hit the underneath of your boot with their pole.

Once the sole of your boot is snow-free, you can put your ski on. The front of the boot goes in first – the little ledge that sticks out from the front of the boot fits into the front of the binding.

Figure 6: putting the front of the boot into the front of the binding

Then make sure the heel is lined up correctly, and press it down firmly. (You don't need to stamp). As you push the heel down, the back of the binding will spring up. That's it, you're in!

Figure 7: ski boot in the ski binding

Do the same for the other ski.

By the way: putting your skis back on after a fall

The back of the ski binding should be in the 'down' position before you put the ski on, then it will be in the 'up' position when you've put the ski on. If you have a fall and your skis come off, the backs of the bindings may well still be 'up'. Push them back down before you put your skis on again.

By the way: putting your skis on on a slope

If you have to put your skis on on a slope, make sure that they are across the slope, not pointing up or downhill – otherwise you'll slide as soon as you put them on. Start with the downhill ski.

If you stand above the skis, it can be hard to get your foot at a suitable angle to go into the binding, especially if the slope is steep. To solve this, stand beneath your skis, and do the crossover – cross your lower leg over the upper one, and put your boot into the binding. You should find that it's at the right angle to go into the binding easily.

Figure 8: putting your skis on on a slope using the 'crossover' technique

Taking your skis off

When it's time to take your skis off, this is done using your ski pole. Push the back of the binding down, and as you do so, lift your heel. Your foot will come free.

Figure 9: taking skis off

You can then take your other ski off in the same way, using a ski pole, or you can push the back of the binding down with the heel of your free boot.

Common faults: using one ski to release the other ski's binding

Some people push the back of one binding down with the tail of their other ski. Although this isn't quite a fault, it's bad practice, because you might damage the base and edges of your ski. It's better to look after your skis, and make sure they only come into contact with snow, and nothing harder. For similar reasons, skiing on a road is best avoided, because any snow-cover is probably patchy.

By the way: names of parts of the skis

It can be useful to know the names of the different parts of your skis. Some of them are shown on this diagram:

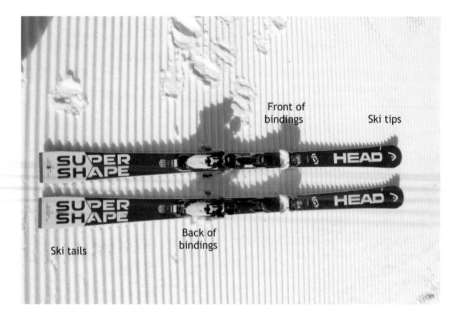

Figure 10: names of parts of the skis

The sides of the skis are called 'the side walls'. If you turn your skis over, you'll see the bases, which are often are black, and the metal edges.

Figure 11: ski bases

The ski brakes are part of the bindings. They are designed to be in a 'down' position when you're not wearing the skis, which stops the skis sliding away without you (hence the name 'brakes').

Figure 12: ski brakes preventing a ski from sliding away

When you put your boots into the ski bindings, the ski brakes are pushed into the 'up' position and now the skis can slide.

The other function of ski brakes is to allow the skis to fit snugly together for carrying. Slide the skis together and you should hear a click as the brakes gently lock, one set under and the other over. (This may not always happen with cheap or worn-out skis, where the brakes are bent out of shape).

Knowing which set of brakes is underneath, and which is on top, is important when carrying skis. It will make the difference between the skis staying together or sliding apart. Carrying your skis is a subject dealt with as a 'by the way' in the next chapter.

Figure 13: the skis fitting together (one set of ski brakes under and the other over)

Now that you know how to put your equipment on, it's time to start skiing.

2 SNOWPLOUGH

Learning to ski usually starts with a snowplough. You may spend the next part of your skiing career trying to get rid of your snowplough, so why do it in the first place? Because it's a relatively simple move, which allows you to control your speed. With an effective snowplough, you won't tear away down to the bottom of the valley. It will give you the control you need to learn skiing fundamentals like turning left and right.

Figure 14: standing still in a snowplough

11

Make a snowplough with your skis by pushing your feet apart, and turning them inwards, so that there's a small gap between the tips of the skis, and the tails of the skis are wide apart. The skis will naturally rest slightly on their inside edges (and you rest on the insides of your feet, where your arches and big toes are).

Standing still in a snowplough

On a gentle slope, it should be quite easy to make your snowplough wide enough so that you can face down the hill, but stay still and not slide. Figure 14 shows the width of plough needed to stand still on that slope.

Common faults: standing still in a snowplough

Not making a wide enough snowplough will result in sliding down the hill rather than standing still.

Snowploughing in a straight line

The next step is to slide down the hill in a straight line, in a snowplough.

In order to get going, bring your feet closer together, so the snowplough becomes narrower. If necessary (this will depend on how steep the slope is), push yourself forward with your poles.

Figure 15: snowploughing in a straight line (a gliding plough)

Once you get going, you can vary the width of the snowplough as necessary, so you travel at just the right speed: if you feel as though you're going too fast, push the tails of the skis out to make a wider plough and slow down; if you grind to a halt, let your skis come closer together, and if necessary, give yourself a little push with your poles.

Note that keeping your skis in a snowplough shape requires some effort. If you relax and do nothing, the skis will naturally come parallel. You have to use your leg muscles to resist this.

Hold your ski poles at about waist height but away from your body, with the poles pointing slightly out and back.

Common faults: snowploughing in a straight line

- Too narrow a snowplough, so your speed runs out of control
- Making too wide a snowplough so you can't get going: it's best to start moving first, then go into a snowplough, and regulate your speed by varying the width of the plough
- A lopsided snowplough: with one ski turned more than the other, or one ski on its edge more than the other. The result? Disaster! No, not really, but you'll probably go off to one side, rather than travelling in a straight line. That's great if you're trying to turn, but not so good if it happens by accident when you're intending to ski in a straight line
- Looking down too much. It's natural to want to check on your skis at first, and that's fine, but you shouldn't look down all the time. Just glance down occasionally to see if your skis are where you want them to be, and the rest of the time, look up. You ski better when you look where you're going, and crash into things less often

Figure 16: looking up in a snowplough

13

Exercise: varying the width of your plough

Figure 17: straight skis to snowplough

A useful exercise at this stage is to practise making your snowplough wider and narrower as you go down the slope. As you push out into a wider plough, you will slow down or stop; as you let your feet come closer together and your snowplough gets narrower, you'll speed up.

Figure 18: snowplough to straight skis

The benefits of a solid snowplough

A solid snowplough is an essential foundation for the early stages of learning to ski.

Later in your skiing career, when you're capable of skiing parallel, you'll still use a snowplough from time to time. For example, when you ski up to the chairlift queue, there may be lots of people around, and no space to turn. A snowplough will come in useful to stop in a straight line.

Mastering the snowplough in a straight line is something to smile about!

Figure 19: mastering the snowplough in a straight line is something to smile about

By the way: how to get up if you fall over

In Chapter 1 I joked that a fall was unlikely, but really a few tumbles are part of learning to ski. If you do fall over, you'll need to know how to get up again.

With your skis off

Ski bindings are designed to release in the event of a high-speed crash, particularly if there's a twisting force. (The force needed to make them release depends on the bindings' setting: the ski hire shop sets the bindings according to your weight and ability, so for example a light beginner's ski bindings would be on a low/loose setting).

If your skis come off, getting up is easy. Just remember to push the backs of your bindings down before you put your skis on again.

With your skis still on

If you fall at low speed, your skis may well stay on. How do you stand up again?

First, your skis must be below you, and across the slope. If they aren't already, try to hotch them round so they are (without trapping your ski pole underneath them as you move).

If you're feeling adventurous, you could lift your legs up in the air, and spin round on your back like a break dancer, until your skis are in the right place.

Once your skis are below you and across the slope, make a fist with your uphill hand, and put it in the snow, ready to push yourself up.

Figure 20: starting position for getting up

Use your uphill hand to push yourself up.

Figure 21: pushing yourself up with the uphill hand

(The steeper the slope, the easier it is to push yourself up, because you start from a position which is closer to upright).

When your bum is over the backs of the skis, you're halfway up.

Figure 22: halfway up

From here, you may be able to stand up. It can be helpful to put your hands on your knees as you do so. Otherwise, you can always ask a friend to give you a hand up from there.

If you're talented enough, you may be able to get up without sitting over the back of your skis first.

Figure 23: getting up

If you can't get up using the method I've explained, an alternative is to take off one ski, preferably the uphill ski, by pushing the back of the binding down with your hand and shaking your heel loose. It's easier to stand up when one foot is ski-free.

By the way: how to carry your skis

Carrying your skis can be a struggle when you're a beginner. It's one of those little things that people just assume you know, and don't explain. A good reason to carry your skis properly is that it takes less effort.

Indoors, or in a crowded area, you should carry your skis upright, as in the photo below.

Figure 24: holding the skis upright

To carry the skis upright, hold the front of the binding (see Figure 24). As I explained in Chapter 1, the ski brakes slot together, one set under, the other over. Hold the binding on the side where the brakes are underneath rather than on top – that way, the skis won't slide apart.

Common faults: carrying your skis upright
- Holding the skis upside down (tails at the top and tips at the bottom)
- Holding the bindings on the side where the brakes are on top, so the skis slide apart

When you're outdoors with plenty of space around you, you can carry the skis over your shoulder.

Figure 25: carrying skis over the shoulder

The skis rest on your shoulder; you hold the skis near the front, so that they balance nicely. The fronts of the bindings sit behind your shoulder.

Figure 26: front of the binding behind the shoulder

Again, make sure the brakes are the correct way round – so that the top ski can't slide forward, but is held in place by the brakes.

Common faults: carrying your skis over your shoulder

- Skis back to front (tails at the front and tips at the back)
- The wrong ski on top, so that brakes don't hold them together and the top ski can slide forward; the solution is to twizzle them 180 degrees so the other ski is on top

By the way: how to get back up the hill

In the initial stages of learning to snowplough, you'll be using a short, gentle slope. When you've skied down it, you need to get back up it again.

The duck walk

Figure 27: the duck walk

To get up a slight gradient, you can do the duck walk. Make a reverse snowplough (tips apart, tails close together), and grip with the inside edges of your skis. Then take little steps up the hill. Use your poles to help. Put them in the snow next to your feet – if you reach further forward than that, you get less leverage.

Common faults: the duck walk

- Not getting onto the inside edges of the skis, but leaving them flat so they don't grip. Think of making your knees go in slightly, to

edge and grip

- Poles in between the skis, not outside. It's quite surprising how often this unorthodox technique is attempted!

Side-stepping

Figure 28: side-stepping up a gentle slope

If the slope is too steep for the duck walk, turn your skis across the slope, and take sideways steps, gripping with the uphill edges of the skis.

Figure 29: side-stepping up a gentle slope

'Across the slope' means at 90 degrees to the fall line. The fall line is directly down the hill – the line a satsuma would take if you let it roll. (If you don't like satsumas, any other roughly spherical object will do).

Common faults: side-stepping

- Stepping a ski up the hill, and resting on its inside/downhill edge, not its uphill edge. This is more likely to happen when the slope is shallow; on a steeper slope, the skis will naturally rest on the correct edges
- Failing to keep the skis across the slope. You have to stay sideways on to the slope. People (especially children) sometimes gradually turn and face uphill. They then slide backwards

By the way: magic carpet lifts

These are really travelators, but 'magic carpet' sounds more exotic.

As a beginner, it can be tiring getting back up the hill using the duck walk or side-stepping. That's why you'll want to start using lifts as soon as you can. Often, there are magic carpets by the beginners' slopes.

At the bottom of the magic carpet, line your skis up straight and give yourself a little push with your poles, onto the moving carpet. Expect to move with the carpet, rather than being surprised, hoping your skis will go off without you (they won't), and falling backwards. Stand on the carpet with your skis parallel, until you get to the top.

Figure 30: reaching the top of the magic carpet

At the top, go straight ahead off the end of the carpet. You can steady yourself with your poles as you slide onto the snow. Ski down the little ramp, and move away from the arrival area quickly - there could be other people coming up behind you.

3 SNOWPLOUGH TURNS

Mastering the snowplough should have given you a reassuring feeling of control.
Once you feel comfortable, and confident that you're not going to slide away to your doom(!), it's time to move on. This could be after just a few attempts at snowploughing in a straight line, or it could take quite a bit longer.

The next challenge is to learn to turn. After all, skiing is a sport of turns – left and right.

Ideally, you'll be on a slope with a shallow gradient – probably the same one you used for snowploughing in a straight line. Start in exactly the same way as before, by standing still in a snowplough. Get moving by making your snowplough narrower, and giving yourself a little push with your poles if necessary.

Once you're moving, start to turn, while staying in a snowplough to control your speed.

Which is the important ski in a turn?
The important ski in a turn is the outside ski (the ski which is on the outside of the curve you're making). It's the left ski when you're turning right – as in the photo collage in Figure 31 below.

Figure 31: a snowplough turn to the skier's right (sequence is right to left)

The right ski is the outside ski when you're turning left, as in the photo collage in Figure 32.

Figure 32: a snowplough turn to the skier's left (sequence is left to right)

The outside ski in a turn is sometimes called 'the turning ski'.
It's worth remembering this – that the outside ski is the important one

in a turn – and getting it straight in your head which ski it is in any turn. That's because the importance of the outside ski runs all the way through skiing, from first-day beginner to World Cup racer.

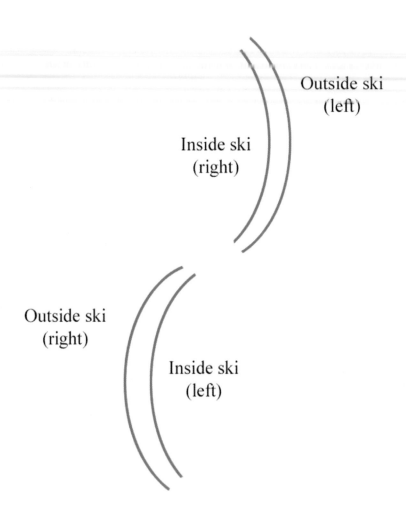

Figure 33: diagram showing outside ski & inside ski

If you imagine a rugby player making a jinking, slaloming run to avoid opposition defenders, he or she pushes off the left leg to move right, and off the right leg to move left. That's a similar idea to ski turns.

As you can see from the diagram (Figure 33), the outside ski changes with every turn.

How do you turn?

It's all very well me saying that the outside ski is the important one, but how do you actually use it to turn?

In order to turn right, press on the left ski, and point it where you want to go; to turn left, press on the right ski, and point it where you want to go. You'll soon get a feel for it.

That's it, put simply. There is a more technical explanation, though, of the elements of a turn.

The elements of a turn

There are three main elements to a snowplough turn. They are:

- Pressure. The outside ski (or turning ski) must be weighted, so it applies pressure to the snow. If it isn't weighted, it won't do the work of turning
- Edge. The outside ski must be tilted slightly onto its inside edge. It's the metal edge of the ski which grips and allows you to turn. If the ski is flat on its base, it will just glide over the snow, and you won't turn
- Rotation. This is the directional element. As you slide, you turn the outside ski and point it where you want to go. In snowplough turns, you can think of pointing both skis in the direction you want to travel

Pressure

Apply pressure to the outside ski by pushing it against the snow with your leg.

Edge

Again using your leg, tip the outside ski slightly onto its edge so it can grip and turn. It's a question of finding the right amount of edge. If you edge the ski too much, it will be difficult to turn.

The inside ski can be just on its inside edge, or more or less flat on the snow.

Figure 34: snowplough turn with inside ski more or less flat on the snow

Rotation

It's by turning the skis, particularly the outside ski, that you actually change direction. Since your foot is attached to the ski via your boot and binding, it's your foot and leg which must turn the ski.

When doing snowplough turns, turn only part way across the slope (say 45 degrees away from the fall line). Go further across a slope with any steepness to it in a snowplough, and you'll force your inside (uphill) leg into an awkward and uncomfortable position.

At this stage, most of your speed control comes from your snowplough, not your turns.

Exercise: outside hand down

An exercise to make sure your weight is on the outside ski can be useful here, for the pressure element of the turn. When turning right, as in the Figure 35 below, reach the outside hand (the left hand) down, and feel your weight come onto the outside (the left) ski. When turning left, reach the outside hand (the right hand) down for the same effect.

As you're doing this exercise, don't forget about edge and rotation. In particular, make sure that you still edge the outside ski as you're reaching the outside hand down – don't let it go flat on its base.

Figure 35: outside hand down

Common faults: snowplough turns

- Forgetting to do a snowplough. Often, the first time someone tries to turn, they concentrate so hard on turning that they forget to snowplough. This can result in going too fast and running out of control
- Edging the outside ski too much. The outside ski has to be on its inside edge a little bit in order to grip, but if you tip it too much onto its edge (too big an edge angle), it will get stuck pointing in one direction, and be difficult to turn
- Not edging the outside ski (enough). If the outside ski isn't edged at all, or only very slightly, it won't grip and so you won't turn. Sometimes this results from a lop-sided snowplough, with the outside ski too flat, and the inside ski edged too much
- Trying to turn with the upper body/shoulders. It's the skis that turn, and your feet are attached to them via your boots and ski bindings; therefore, it should be the feet and legs which turn the skis. Trying to turn using the upper body/shoulders doesn't work well, and tends to throw your weight onto the wrong ski

Figure 36: the mistake of turning with the upper body first

Surprising as it may seem, the performance depicted in the photo above was achieved without any formal training in the dramatic arts.

By the way: wearing pole straps

Your ski poles have straps, which you can wear if you want – but you don't have to.

If you let go of a pole handle and you're not wearing the strap, you'll drop your pole. Do so at high speed, and by the time you've stopped you'll have a long walk back up the slope to fetch it. If you're racing giant slalom, you'll record a terrible time.

On the other hand, if you're snowploughing on the nursery slope, it won't matter much if you drop your pole – you can just pick it up again.

If you decide to use your pole straps, there's a correct way to put them on. First, put your hand through the strap, palm facing down.

Figure 37: putting hand through pole strap

Then lift your thumb up and back so it is over the top of the pole strap.

Figure 38: thumb up and back, over pole strap

Finally, with the strap under your thumb, grasp the pole handle.

Figure 39: holding the pole strap and pole handle

If you're holding the pole strap in this way and you fall, the strap won't pull on your wrist and hurt it. If you wear the strap but don't hold it like this, there's a risk you could hurt your wrist in a fall. How often this risk materialises in practice, I don't know.

By the way: greens, blues, reds and blacks

Once you've mastered snowplough turns, you're ready for an easy green run.

In ascending order of difficulty, runs are classed green, blue, red and black. These categories are a reasonably good guide, but there's some variation within categories from country to country and resort to resort. Even in the same resort one green could be slightly more challenging than another; and the same run could be easier in the morning when it's just been groomed, and harder in the afternoon.

If you take lessons with a local ski instructor, they will know exactly where to go, according to your level and the conditions.

You'll probably need to take a chairlift to get to the top of the green run.

By the way: using a chairlift

Figure 40: Cascades chairlift, Val Thorens

To use the chairlift, you have to buy a ski pass (sometimes called a lift pass or lift ticket).

Most ski resorts now have ski passes which are read automatically at a turnstile (see * at the end of this chapter for more).

Keep your ski pass in a left hand pocket. The small pocket towards the bottom of the left sleeve is ideal, if your jacket has one. Your ski pass will be recognised by the pass reader without you having to take it out of your pocket, and the turnstile will allow you through.

(If the pass reader doesn't recognize your ski pass and the turnstile won't let you through, it could be because your ski pass is in the same pocket as a mobile phone, credit card, or an old ski pass. These items interfere with the signal, and prevent the machine from reading your ski pass).

Once you've gone through the turnstile, you should take your pole straps off. If you're still wearing the straps while you ride the chairlift and your poles get caught up in the machinery, you could hurt your wrists. I've never seen this happen in practice, but it's the reason usually given for taking pole straps off.

Figure 41: going through the turnstile to a chairlift

When you get to the front of the queue, there are little barriers which open at the right moment, to let you through.

Figure 42: barriers at Plein Sud chairlift, Val Thorens

When the barriers open, go forward as far as you can, to a stop sign or the end of the matting. The chairlift will come from behind you, and when it touches the back of your legs, sit down on it.

Most modern chairlifts are designed to slow down at the start (loading) and finish (unloading) points, making it easier and more comfortable to get on and off. Chairlifts of this design are called 'detachable', because the chair detaches from the wire during loading and unloading, and a different, slower system moves it along. There are still a few non-detachable chairlifts, which remain attached to the wire all the time. Because they don't slow down at the loading point, they bash the back of your legs as you get on. Since they're one-speed, they travel at a leisurely pace to the top.

You'll probably be on the lift with other people – chairlifts usually take four or six skiers/snowboarders. There are still some older chairs for three, two, or even only one person.

Figure 43: one-seat chairlift on display in Les Menuires

As you set off, look along at the other people on the chair and carefully and gradually bring down the safety bar. If you pull it down abruptly, you risk bashing a fellow passenger on the head – someone who is leaning forward to adjust their boot, or somebody who is sitting forward because they are wearing a rucksack.

Once the safety bar is down, there's a foot rest for you to put your feet/skis on. While on the chairlift, hold both poles in one hand, about a third of the way down from the handles. Relax and enjoy the ride until you're near the arrival point.

As you approach the arrival point, take your skis off the foot rest, and lift up the safety bar. A sign may prompt you to do so. If not, lift the bar as you pass the last pylon before the end, and that should be about right.

Figure 44: lifting up the bar

Keep both poles in one hand right to the end, then you'll be able to use your other hand on the chair to help you stand up.

Figure 45: ready to get off, both poles still in one hand

There's a point where your skis touch the ground, and at that moment, stand up and ski straight forwards with parallel skis.

Figure 46: getting off the chairlift at the top

Don't do a snowplough as you go down the snowy ramp from the lift, because the tails of your skis could get caught up with those of the person next to you; don't try to turn if there's someone next to you, since they might not want to go the same way as you. Don't take a pole in each hand as you stand up and start pushing with them, as your poles may get caught under the chair.

Common faults: getting onto the chairlift

- Failing to move far enough forward when the little barriers open. The chair comes round the corner, then straightens up. It is easy to sit on if you've moved forward to the end of the loading area. If you haven't moved forward to the right place, it will come at you from the side and may knock you over

- Unbalancing the chair. If not all the places are taken, try to balance up the chair, rather than all sitting on one side. You have to think about this when getting on, because once you're under way and the safety bar is down, it's probably too late to move

Figure 47: unbalanced chair

Common faults: riding the chairlift

- Digging your elbows into your neighbour's ribs. On a full chair, there may not be much space. Try to sit with your arms slightly forward, otherwise your elbows may make it an uncomfortable ride for the person next to you

- Smoking. If you're sharing a chair with strangers, don't smoke. Never puff away in the lift queue either – after all, it's not 1990 any more
- Swinging your leg. If you sit on the chair swinging your leg, it makes the whole chair swing, which can be annoying for your fellow passengers

Common faults: getting off the chairlift

Sometimes first-time chairlift riders are nervous about the arrival point. If you're hesitant and half-hearted when getting off the chair, and you secretly hope that your skis will go off without you, you might well fall backwards. Instead, stand up with conviction, and stay over your skis. As long as you believe you're going to stand up, and do it, you'll be fine.

The only thing we have to fear is...fear itself, as Franklin D Roosevelt might have said in this circumstance, if he had ever been a ski instructor. He would have made sure you didn't get into a great depression about getting off the chairlift - and that you didn't make a great depression in the snow by falling over.

*Ski pass readers at the turnstiles

Figure 48: ski pass readers at turnstiles

My brother Andrew, who knows about these things, tells me that ski passes and ski pass readers at the turnstile work using something called NFC (Near Field Communications). 'There's a coil (small and rather flat) built into the ski pass, which receives radio waves from the reader. The radio waves generate a tiny amount of electrical current in the coil, which is used to power a little chip in the card with your details in it. There is enough power for the chip to transmit a reply to the reader. An earlier variant of the technology called RFID (radio frequency ID), was entirely passive – the reader could get fixed information back from the card, but it couldn't have a 'conversation' to allow authenticating, say for access to one lift but not another.'

By the way: using your poles as brakes in the lift queue

Figure 49: using poles as brakes

In general, you shouldn't use your poles as brakes - speed control comes from your skis. One exception to this rule is in the lift queue. When there are lots of people around, there may not be space to do a turn or a snowplough, and if there's a little down slope, you could slide into the person ahead of you. Instead of making new friends in this unorthodox way, put your hands on top of your poles (or in the straps like Marina), and the points of the poles in the snow near the tips of your skis. In this position, you can use your poles as brakes to stop yourself sliding forwards.

4 PLOUGH PARALLELS

Plough parallel turns are an intermediate step on the way to parallel skiing. You start these turns in a snowplough, and finish them parallel.

Begin your turn as before in a snowplough.

Figure 50: snowplough at the start of a plough parallel turn (sequence left to right)

Continue round the turn until your skis begin to steer across the slope near the end of the turn. At this point, allow your feet to come closer together, and let the skis run parallel.

Figure 51: bringing the skis parallel at the end of the turn (sequence right to left)

Weight on the outside ski

It's the inside ski which moves closer to the outside ski. To achieve this, more of your weight must be on the outside ski at the end of the turn. The inside ski is therefore lighter, and can move towards the outside ski, rather than being weighted and stuck.

The next turn in the series

To start the next turn, make a snowplough shape with the new outside ski, and towards the end of the turn, allow your feet to come closer together and the skis parallel. The turns continue like that – snowplough at the start, and parallel at the end.

Sequential movements

In plough parallel turns, the movements of the skis happen one after the other - sequentially rather than simultaneously. First, the outside ski changes edge (from outside edge to inside edge) and turns. Then, towards the end of the turn, the inside ski changes edge (from inside edge to outside edge), and steers parallel with the outside ski.

Turn shape and speed control

Ending the turn parallel means you can 'finish off' the turn – i.e. steer the skis round until you're facing sideways across the slope. If you were still in a snowplough, it would be awkward and uncomfortable to steer across the slope; and the snowplough is constantly driving you back into the slope.

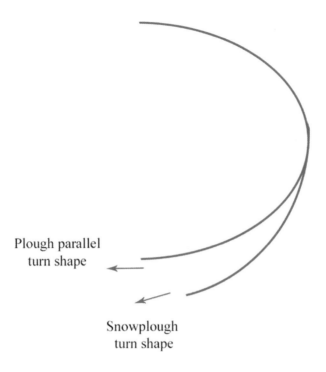

Plough parallel
turn shape

Snowplough
turn shape

Figure 52: turn shape plough vs plough parallel

Until now, your main method of speed control has been the snowplough. Now, you're starting to use turn shape as well. When you turn your skis into the slope, gravity means that you'll accelerate; as you steer your skis sideways across the slope, gravity no longer makes you accelerate, and the forces of resistance mean that you slow down.

In snowplough, you're always using your leg muscles to slow yourself down. By steering your skis sideways across the slope, you're no longer resisting gravity, and you can relax. (Somewhat!)

Because you're now able to steer across the slope, you can ski a slightly steeper slope than you could using snowplough turns.

If you're skiing a pitch that's a little steep for your current skills, you can use a fairly wide snowplough to get round the corner, so that you don't accelerate too much while the skis are pointing down the hill, then steer parallel across. This is a legitimate tactic.

By the way: three methods of speed control

Figure 53: counting the three main methods of speed control

This is a good time to mention the three main methods of speed control. In ski lessons, I sometimes say that there can't be more than three, because I only have three-fingered gloves to count them on. That's my main joke. If I ever change my gloves, I'll have to think of a new one.

At this point in the beginners' progression, you use two of them already – snowplough and turn shape. The third is skidding, and it's used at the end of parallel turns (see Chapter 5).

Common faults: plough parallels

These are some of the mistakes commonly made when starting to do plough parallel turns:

- A very wide a snowplough at the start of the turn can lead to your inside ski getting stuck on its inside edge; it's then difficult to narrow your stance and bring the skis parallel further round the turn. Most of the time, it's better to use a moderate snowplough at the top of the turn

- Twisting and/or tipping the upper body in advance of the skis. This means you trap the inside ski under you. Instead of being light and easy to move, it gets stuck

Figure 54: the mistake of twisting and tipping the upper body into the turn

- Weight split evenly between the two skis, rather than allowing more of it to come onto the outside ski. Again, this makes it harder to move the inside ski closer to and parallel with the outside ski
- Clinging onto a wide stance for reasons of balance. It's true that balancing is easier with a wide base of support (like the Eiffel Tower). Sometimes people find it difficult (physically and/or psychologically) to let go of a wide snowplough stance, and to bring the feet closer together in a narrower parallel stance. Nevertheless, in order to progress, it has to be done

Exercise: lifting the heel of the inside ski

A useful exercise at this stage is lifting the heel of the inside ski at the end of the turn, to ensure your weight is on the outside ski.

Go round the first part of the turn in a snowplough, and as you're skiing across the slope at the end of the turn, lift the heel of your inside (uphill) ski. If you achieve this, most of your weight must be on the outside (downhill) ski, which is where it should be.

Figure 55: lifting the heel of the inside ski at the end of the turn

Also, if you're able to lift the heel of the inside ski, rather than the whole ski or the tip, you must be in a reasonably good middle to forward position on your skis (see 'posture', in the next chapter).

If it's too difficult to lift the heel of your ski and hold it in that position for a second or two, an easier version of this exercise is to tap the heel twice or three times.

Exercise: side-slipping

Direction of travel

Figure 56: side-slipping

Side-slipping involves standing with your skis across a reasonably steep slope, and slipping sideways down it.

Make sure your skis are across the slope – that's to say at 90 degrees to the fall line. (Remember, the fall line is the path a satsuma would follow if it were to roll down the hill).

If, instead of having your skis across the slope, you point the tips slightly down the hill, you'll slide forwards, not sideways; if you point the tails of your skis down the hill, you'll slide backwards. That's why it's vital to keep the skis across the slope for side-slipping. Failing to do so is one of the common faults identified below.

Let's look at side-slipping in detail now – gripping, slipping and stopping.

Gripping

When standing still, your skis must be edged, so that they grip.

Figure 57: edging and gripping to stand still

Slipping

To side-slip, release the edges by flattening the skis. Concentrate on flattening the downhill ski. You'll slide sideways down the hill. Try to keep your upper body facing somewhat down the slope.

Figure 58: side-slipping down the hill

Stopping

When you want to stop side-slipping, edge the skis again.

Figure 59: stop side-slipping by gripping with the edges

You should practise side-slipping both sides – facing one way, then the other; in other words, with one leg down the hill, then the other leg downhill. Then you won't become a one-sided skier, favouring one leg over the other.

Common faults: side-slipping

Two things are quite likely to happen when you first side-slip:

- Catching the uphill ski on its downhill (inside) edge. When you flatten your skis, you should nevertheless keep them just on their uphill edges. It's easy to let your uphill ski go too far and change onto its inside edge. This will almost certainly happen if you allow your feet to drift apart. If the uphill ski catches, you won't be able to side-slip

Figure 60: catching the inside edge of the uphill ski when side-slipping

- Failing to keep the skis across the slope and snowploughing. If you allow the ski tips to point down the slope, you start to slide forwards, instead of sideways down the hill. The inexperienced side-slipper often reacts to this by going into a snowplough to halt their forward momentum. That's a mistake. The move you should make to prevent yourself going forwards is a twist of both skis, to bring them back to 90 degrees to the fall line

The benefits of side-slipping

I said those two faults were 'quite likely' to happen. In fact, when side-slipping for the first time, it's 99% certain that's what's going to happen - but trial and error is the only way, and it's worth doing.

Why? When side-slipping, you no longer rest on the two inside edges of the skis, as in a snowplough; instead, you're on the parallel edges of your skis (left and left, or right and right, depending on which way you're facing).

Figure 61: snowplough edges and parallel edges

Starting to feel comfortable on the parallel edges is good practice for the next step in the progression, parallel skiing.

Also, side-slipping is very similar to skidding. Both involve travelling with the skis turned sideways to your direction of travel: in side-slipping, gravity is the force making you move, whereas in skidding you turn your skis sideways while moving along, and your own momentum keeps you going.

Skidding is a key speed-control method at the end of a parallel turn. Now is a great time to get a feel for it.

Exercise: skidding

The best terrain for a first attempt at skidding is a bank at the side of the piste – a sideways slope or camber. That's because, if you turn and edge your skis up the bank, they fall naturally onto their parallel edges. (To edge them down the bank is harder because there's further to go to get them onto their edges).

Figure 62: skidding on a bank

Set off in a straight line to take a little speed, then turn your skis up the bank, but keep going in your original direction. If you do this, the skis will be turned across your direction of travel – i.e. skidding sideways. In the photo above, Marina is travelling towards the camera, where her head and shoulders are facing, not where her skis are pointing.

If you can get good at skidding, you'll be relaxed about parallel skiing, because you'll know how to slow down at the end of each turn, and how to stop without going back to snowplough.

Common faults: skidding

These mistakes are often made when trying to skid for the first time:

- Setting off in a snowplough. If you set off in a snowplough, your inside ski has to change edges before it can skid, and it may get stuck on the wrong edge. If instead you set off with your skis parallel and flat, it will be easy to turn them both at the same time
- Turning both skis but edging them too much. If when you turn your skis, you edge them a lot, they'll grip and take you in the direction they are pointing, instead of skidding. For successful skidding, the skis should be edged just a little
- Sliding backwards. If you turn the skis too far up the bank, when you slow down you'll start sliding backwards. Instead, turn the skis enough, but not too much – like Marina.

If you do find yourself sliding backwards, this is what to do: make a backwards snowplough, and steer your skis back across the slope. Try not to steer them further towards the fall line, as you'll accelerate (then probably fall over).

Now that your skis are parallel at least at the end of your turns, and you've learnt some of the skills you'll need, it's time to have a go at parallel turns.

5 PARALLEL TURNS

Everything so far has been leading to this: parallel turns. They are at the end of the beginner's progression. If you can master parallel turns, you can justifiably say that you're no longer a beginner.

Figure 63: parallel skiing

You already finish your turns parallel, so it's the way you start your turns that needs to change.

The difference between plough parallel and parallel

A plough parallel turn starts with a movement of the outside ski only. It changes edge, and it turns, creating a plough or wedge shape in relation to the other ski. Only later does the inside ski change edge and steer parallel with the outside ski.

In parallel turns, the satellite delay between one ski and the other is eliminated: both skis change edges and turn at the same time.

How to make a parallel turn

To initiate a parallel turn, move your weight onto the outside ski at the start of the turn. This can be by an extension of your outside leg: stand onto the outside ski.

The result is that your inside ski is light at the start of the turn, instead of being weighted and stuck. It should be easy to make it change edges at the same time as the outside ski, and steer parallel with it.

Keep your skis parallel as you steer round the turn.

At the end of the turn, control your speed using turn shape and skidding.

To start the next turn, transfer your weight from the outside ski on the old turn to the outside ski on the new turn, and the process begins again - changing edges of both skis at the same time, steering the skis parallel round the turn, and controlling your speed at the end of the turn.

The elements of a parallel turn

These, then, are the essential elements of a parallel turn:

- A weight transfer from the old outside ski to the new outside ski
- Both skis change edges at the same time (more or less simultaneous with the weight transfer)
- The skis stay parallel as you steer them round the turn
- Speed control using turn shape and skidding

There are further elements:

- A parallel turn is not so tight as a plough parallel turn, so you will have travelled further down the slope by the time it is finished
- As a result of a less tight turn shape, you go a little faster
- Because you're going faster, you can lean in order to edge the skis

Let's take a look at some of those elements in more detail.

Weight transfer

Figure 64: initiation of a parallel turn with weight transfer (sequence right to left)

The photo sequence above shows a weight transfer from the old outside ski (the left ski), to the new outside ski (the right ski).

The weight transfer is usually achieved by extending the legs – they are flexed at the end of the old turn, and you extend them to start the new turn. As you do so, you stand onto the new outside ski.

In the final photo of the sequence above, the tail of Marina's inside ski has come off the snow. That's not essential, or even necessarily something to aim for, but it neatly demonstrates that, at that point in the turn, her weight is on the other ski.

Up and down movement

There are differing opinions about up and down movement. Some instructors introduce it at an early stage and emphasize its importance, but that comes with a risk of encouraging movements made for the sake of it, rather than to a purpose. It can be quite difficult for relative beginners to get up and down movement right, and if the movements are slightly mistimed, they won't contribute to good skiing.

Other instructors point out that you can move your weight from one leg to the other with negligible vertical movement. They argue for the other extreme, of eliminating up and down movement as much as possible.

I suggest that on a perfectly-groomed piste, only a little up and down movement is needed; in chopped up snow, more vertical movement is useful, to lighten the skis and help them change edges without getting caught in the snow.

When you get the hang of the weight transfer to start a new turn, you should find it gives you rhythm: you can say to yourself, *hup*, onto the left ski, *hup*, onto the right ski, *hup* onto the left ski, and so on.

Edge change

Figure 65: edged to flat (sequence right to left)

In parallel skiing, both skis change edges at the same time, rather than one then the other.

The images above (Figure 65) show the change from edged skis to flat skis at the end of one turn; the images below (Figure 66) show the change from flat skis to edged skis to start the next turn.

Figure 66: flat to edged (sequence right to left)

Parallel skis

In parallel turns, the skis stay parallel all the time.

Also, both skis should have the same edge angle. To achieve this, keep your shins parallel. This means that one knee (the outside knee) is angled in a little, and the other knee (the inside knee) is angled out a little.

Generally, the 'knee in' movement is easy, but some people struggle to make the 'knee out' movement. Instead of parallel shins, they make an A shape (as in the right hand photo in Figure 67 below). Then, the skis aren't edged equally, and there's a risk of the inside ski catching on its inside edge towards the end of the turn, instead of skidding on its outside edge.

(Technically, the knee is a hinge joint which can't move sideways in isolation; the knee in and knee out movements are actually coming from a rotation of the femur in the hip joint).

Figure 67: parallel shins vs not parallel shins

Turn shape, speed, and speed control

A parallel turn isn't as tight as a plough parallel turn. If you do a snowplough at the start of the turn, it enables you to get round the corner while going only a little way down the slope. A parallel turn is more smooth and rounded, and typically you'll be further down the slope at the end of it.

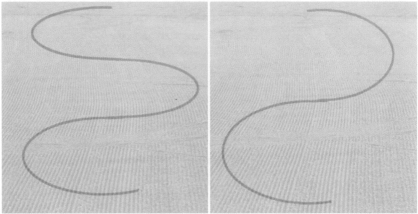

Figure 68: plough parallel turn shape vs parallel turn shape

You also take more speed in a parallel turn. This is partly because a speed control method (the snowplough) has been taken away; and partly because in a less tight turn, your skis are pointing down the hill for a longer distance, so you accelerate more.

You have to accept the extra speed.

To an extent, it's a matter of perception. What seems fast to an inexperienced skier won't necessarily seem fast to a more experienced skier. Video can help here: if you get a friend to film you, when you watch it back, you'll get a realistic idea of how fast you're going (or not).

It's also relative to your skills. You'll be happy to point your skis down the hill and accelerate in the middle of the turn if you're confident that you can control your speed (by steering across the slope and skidding) at the end of the turn.

Whee-whoa turns

This idea of acceleration and speed control at different points in the turn is sometimes described as making 'whee–whoa' turns. As you point your skis down the hill and accelerate, you say to yourself 'wheeeeee!'; then as you control your speed at the end of the turn, you say 'whooooaaa!'.

Turn shape depends on gradient

The turn shape you should choose depends on the gradient of the slope. If it's a gentle slope, you can end your turn going diagonally down and across the slope, because not too much speed control is needed. These are sometimes called open turns. On a steeper slope, it's a good idea to finish off the turn – i.e. to steer all the way round until your skis are facing across the slope – because more speed control is required.

Skidding

Figure 69: skidding at the end of a turn

Skidding is achieved by pushing the tails of the skis round at the end of the turn. This may cause the snow to spray up. You can decide how much skidding to do, according to how steep the slope is, and how much you want to slow down.

Lean

Figure 70: leaning to edge the skis

You have to lean in order to put your skis on their parallel edges. The extra speed in parallel turns generates the forces (centripetal forces) that allow you to lean but not fall over.

Ideally, your legs will lean into the turn more than your upper body (as in the photo of Marina in Figure 70 above); that helps you stay standing without relying too much on the centripetal forces.

(The idea of leaning the legs into the turn more than the upper body has two technical names: 'angulation' and 'lateral separation'. They both mean the same thing. You don't need to remember these names as long as you understand the idea, but it may be helpful to recognise them in case someone else uses these terms).

Exercise: outside hand down

A parallel skis version of the 'outside hand down' exercise described in Chapter 3 is a good way to practise leaning the legs into the turn more than the upper body.

Figure 71: a parallel turn version of the 'outside hand down' exercise

The parallel turn as a whole

Figure 72: a basic parallel turn to the skier's right

We've looked at the elements of a basic parallel turn, but it will be helpful to see what it looks like as a whole. Above (Figure 72) is a turn to the skier's right, and below (Figure 73) is a turn to the skier's left.

Figure 73: a basic parallel turn to the skier's left

Exercise: falling leaf

Falling leaf is a useful exercise at this stage. It is a variant of side-slipping (see Chapter 4), but instead of simply slipping sideways down the slope (try saying that out loud!), you go forwards and backwards too.

Start with your skis across the slope, but point your ski tips slightly down the hill. You should go forwards and sideways.

Then twist both skis to point the tails slightly down the hill, and you'll go backwards and sideways.

Continue in this way – forwards, backwards, forwards, backwards - with an element of side-slip down the hill too. Keep doing it until you've really got the hang of it and you feel relaxed and in control.

The falling leaf in Figure 74 below shows backwards, forwards, backwards, forwards – but the principle is exactly the same.

Figure 74: falling leaf

Uphill pole plant

Some people find it difficult to go backwards. Often the barrier is more psychological than physical. One thing that can help is an uphill pole plant.

Figure 75: uphill pole plant in falling leaf

When changing from forwards to backwards, reach the uphill pole forward and touch it in the snow. It provides a pivot-point, which helps you twist the skis to point the tails down the hill. It can also steady you and help with balance.

(It's best not to put the downhill pole in the snow, because you may trip over it).

If you can overcome any mental block about going backwards and commit to falling leaf, it will really help your skiing.

One benefit is that it gets you twisting both skis at the same time - a skill that is needed in parallel turns.

Also, people who are new to parallel turns are sometimes disinclined to push the tails of the skis far enough round at the end of the turn. Instead they finish the turn with their skis facing diagonally down and across the hill. As a result, they miss out on skidding, and on some turn shape, and don't get the speed control they should. They tend to ski too far across the slope at the end of the turn.

If you do a lot of falling leaf, you learn to push the tails of the skis round without being fearful of the consequences. Then you trust your ability to do so in parallel turns too, and skid with confidence.

Like side-slipping, falling leaf should be practised both sides – i.e. facing one way then the other. In other words, do the exercise with your right leg down the hill, then do it with your left leg down the hill (or vice versa).

Common faults: falling leaf

Many of the mistakes that are made when side-slipping also occur when doing falling leaf. For example, when going forwards it's easy (but wrong) to go into a snowplough, instead of keeping the skis parallel and twisting both of them to slow down then change direction and go backwards.

One fault that's specific to falling leaf is going forwards more than backwards. If you start in the middle of the piste, and end up at the far side, you've probably been going a long way forwards, with confidence and panache, and only a very short way backwards, with timidity and gaucherie.

Exercise: skid to a stop

This is a good time to practise a skid to a stop, too. (A skid to a stop is also known as a 'hockey stop', because of the way ice hockey players stop by turning the blades of their skates sideways to skid and stop.)

A skid to a stop often comes after a series of turns, but it can be a stand-alone exercise, and that's what I'll describe here.

Set off in a straight line down the hill, with parallel skis flat on their bases. Turn your skis sideways, keeping them parallel, and skid without changing direction. Try to keep your head and shoulders facing forward (down the slope), rather than turning them where your skis are pointing.

After skidding for a distance, edge the skis more, to come to a stop.

Figure 76: skid to a stop - straight line, skid, stop

You may have noticed that this is very similar to the skidding exercise described in Chapter 4. The main difference is that now, we're increasing the edge angle at the end, to come to a clean stop.

Common faults: skid to a stop

- Setting off on a curved path, rather than in a straight line. You'll develop your skills more if you meet the challenge that's set and begin by skiing in a straight line down the hill, rather than trying something slightly different because it might be easier
- After turning the skis, veering off to the side rather than skidding in straight line. This could be because you've turned the skis too

gradually – it's better to turn them quite quickly – or because you're edging the skis too much, so they grip and turn

In both exercises - skidding in the last chapter, and skid to a stop here - it is possible (and helpful) to add in a pole plant to initiate the turn of the skis.

By the way: pole plant

A pole plant is really not so much a 'plant' as a light touch of your pole in the snow, to the inside of the turn.

How to pole plant

Figure 77: pole plant

Reach your pole forward, touch it in the snow, and turn your skis to the same side as the pole plant. In other words, plant the right pole when you turn right, and the left pole when you turn left.

The pole plant initiates the turn, so the sequence should be 'reach the pole forward, then touch it in the snow and turn'.

A pole plant should happen at the same time as the leg extension/weight transfer.

It would be worth looking again at the basic parallel turn images under the heading 'the parallel turn as a whole' earlier in this chapter. Check when Marina does her pole plant: for each turn, it's the second photo in the sequence.

The pole points forward when you're about to plant it, but as you turn and ski past the spot where you planted it, it points backwards. As it does so, let it come away from the snow, and try to make sure your hand is in, or returns to, a good basic position - about waist height, and away from your body (forward and out to the side). Don't let your hand get dragged back (see 'common faults', below).

The point of a pole plant

A pole plant is useful for several reasons:

- It gives the skis a point to turn around. This is so, even though it's only a light touch, and the pole is only in the snow for a second or so

- Using your pole as a pivot point in the turn is especially important where there's more resistance to the skis turning – for example when you're *in* soft snow, rather than *on* firm snow – or when you need to turn your skis quickly – for example, in moguls (bumps)

- If you plant the pole well down the hill on a steep slope, it helps you get forward

- It gives you rhythm, especially when doing short turns

- It provides an extra point of balance

Common faults: pole plant

These are a few of the things that sometimes go wrong:

- On very early attempts, people occasionally plant to the outside of the turn, rather than to the inside. It may help to imagine swinging around a lamp post, rather than punting to the outside of your boat on the river Cam

- In a series of turns, the pole plant starts correctly, to the inside of the turn, but the timing goes wrong, for example by doing pole plants at a faster tempo than turns. Then the pole plant can end up being to the outside of the turn

- Too late with the pole plant – starting the turn first, then doing a pole plant as an afterthought. The pole plant should initiate the turn, i.e. come right at the start of it, rather than happen part way through it

- Not reaching forward enough. You should reach the pole towards the tips of your skis (but off to the side, so you don't trip over the pole). If you only aim to plant the pole beside your feet, because you're travelling along your pole plant point will soon be behind you

- Reaching your hand too high in the air, so your pole plant looks exaggerated and odd. The height of Marina's hand in the photo collage above is just right (naturally!)

- Letting your hand and arm get dragged back after the pole plant, either because you didn't reach far enough forward to begin with, or because you left your pole in the snow for too long

Your hands and arms have to move in a pole plant, but it's important that they don't windmill wildly, as this can unbalance you. You should aim for economy of movement – just what's needed, and no more.

Learning to pole plant can be tricky. As with any other new element in your skiing, you have to think about it, and it can feel as though the rest of your skiing is going haywire in the meantime. If you persevere, your pole plant will become automatic, and you can then focus on a different aspect of skiing.

Pole plant: hold vs throw

When you reach the pole forward to plant it, there are two grip options: you can 'hold' the pole handle in your hand, or 'throw' it forward.

Figure 78: pole plant - hold vs throw

If you 'hold', you keep a tight grip on the pole handle all the time, and you advance the pole by bending your wrist and pushing your arm forward. If you 'throw', you open your hand, so that the pole grip is still held between your thumb and forefinger at the top, but is released by the lower part of your hand and it swings forward.

Figure 78 shows hold and throw. (In fact, both photos are of the same pole plant, so in this case 'hold' is just an earlier phase of a 'throw' pole plant).

Either type of pole plant is fine – you can decide which suits you best.

By the way: posture

A snowplough tends to make you sit back, rather than stand in a good skiing posture. That's why posture appears here, in the parallel skiing chapter, not earlier in this book.

A good basic posture for skiing is:

- Feet about hip width apart, so the skis are flat on their bases when standing on level ground
- Slightly flexed ankles, knees, and hips
- Hands about waist height and away from the body – in front and out to the sides
- Poles pointing slightly out and back

- Arms slightly bent at the elbows, and elbows slightly out
- Head up, looking where you're going

The result should be that your weight is over your feet and your bindings, in the middle of the skis.

Figure 79: a good basic posture

Common faults: posture

Many posture faults concern being too far back. If your weight is on the tails of your skis, they won't swish round as you try to do a parallel turn – they'll get stuck instead.

These are some common problems:

- Hands held high up, and hips back
- Often together with high hands, elbows in rather than slightly out
- Not enough ankle flex. If your ankles aren't flexed, your shins will be upright rather than angled forward. If you then bend your knees, you make the shape of the front legs and seat of a chair, and your weight is over the backs of the skis

Figure 80: not enough ankle flex

- Too much bend at the hips/waist, so that you fold in the middle

Figure 81: too much bend at the hips/waist

Aim for a modest and even amount of flex in the three key joints - ankles, knees and hips – and you won't go far wrong.

Posture: forward movement to start each turn

Figure 82: moving forward to start the turn

You shouldn't stay fixed in the good posture described above, like a stone statue. It's a balanced, 'ready to move', starting position.

In particular, there should be some forward and backward movement in every turn.

You move (up and) forward as you start a turn. Why? Because in the middle of the turn, when the skis are pointing down the hill, they're no longer horizontal – they're at the same angle as the slope itself. You move forward to be in a good position relative to the slope and your skis.

As you steer the skis across the slope, you'll naturally come (down and) back to a middle position.

Figure 83: middle position at the end of the turn

Then, make an effort to get forward again to start the next turn.

Posture: further thoughts

Here are three further thoughts on posture:

- Making a move forward to start the turn is all the more important when you're on a steep slope, and of course, you have to move further in order to stay in a good position relative to your skis when they are angled down a steep hill. It can be harder, psychologically, to move forwards on a steep slope, because your natural instinct may be to back away from the drop

- Posture differs depending on whether you're in 'Sunday afternoon cruise' mode, or skiing fast and aggressively. When skiing fast, it's appropriate to adopt a lower, more flexed and more dynamic posture

- Posture may be different depending on the type of skiing you're doing. On an icy race piste, bending more at the hip, so the upper body is forward over the front of the skis, helps them to grip. When skiing bumps or off piste, grip is generally not an issue, and a rather more upright upper body means your legs can act as shock absorbers: when they bend to absorb a bump, if you are more upright in your upper body, you won't get winded!

Figure 84: lower, more dynamic posture when skiing fast

By the way: drag lifts

Figure 85: drag lift

Drag lifts take skiers up the hill one at a time, by pulling them up a track. These lifts are also known as button lifts, and (in North America) platter lifts. The Dutch call them pancake lifts.

They are sometimes referred to as 'Pomas' too. Jean Pomagalski, an engineer of Polish origin, invented the drag lift, and installed the first one at l'Eclose, Alpe d'Huez, in 1936. He went on to found the lift company Poma, which is still going. These days, Poma make and install all kinds of ski lift, but the company name is still most closely associated with drag lifts.

Riding a drag lift

Join the queue for a drag lift, and when it's your turn, you'll see that there's a row of poles with black discs (or buttons or, if you're Dutch, pancakes) attached. The front pole should flop forward, which means it's ready to go. (Sometimes, the front pole has got caught up with others, and it has to be untangled).

Figure 86: getting hold of the drag lift pole

Take the drag lift pole and pull it towards you with one hand. Pulling it against the wand (indicated with a red arrow in Figure 86) is what makes it set off.

Put the pole between your legs, so the disc rests against the back of your thighs. As the pole sets off, stay standing up, and keep your skis parallel.

It's the disc that pulls you up the hill. The French name for this type of lift is *tire-fesses*, which translates literally as 'pull-buttocks'. That should give you a clear idea of how the thing works.

Hold both ski poles in one hand. You can hold the drag lift pole lightly with the other hand. The drag lift will take you to the top of the track.

Figure 87: riding the drag lift

When you get near the top of the track, you'll go over the crest of the hill, then downhill. Wait until you're on the downhill ramp, then take the drag lift pole out from between your legs, and let go of it.

Figure 88: letting go of the drag lift pole

Common faults: drag lifts

- Trying to sit down on the disc, instead of standing up. If you attempt to sit down, you'll sit all the way down onto the snow, and fall over
- After falling over as described above, clinging on to the lift pole, so it drags you up the hill while you're lying on the snow. If you fall over, let go!
- Holding on too tight with your hands. You should be dragged up the slope by the disc pulling on the back of your thighs, not by holding onto the pole with your hands
- At the top, letting go too early, when you're still on the up slope. You'll slide backwards. (If you do find yourself in this position, as with skidding in Chapter 4, do a backwards snowplough, and steer your skis across the slope)

The future of drag lifts

Drag lifts aren't universally popular. Some people find them uncomfortable, and certainly you don't get to rest in the same way as you do on a chairlift. They also require more skill from the user than other types of lift.

What's more, they aren't as efficient as other lifts, in terms of the number of skiers they take to the top of the mountain per hour. A member of lift staff must be present to supervise and help, whereas some newer types of lift are designed to run without any intervention by human beings.

For these reasons, many resorts are taking drag lifts out, and replacing them with chairlifts or other lift types.

For the moment, though, if you do any significant amount of skiing, you'll come across drag lifts – in mountain resorts, on dry slopes, and in indoor snow domes. Riding a drag lift is still an essential skiing skill, and will remain so for the foreseeable future.

Beyond basic parallel turns

Parallel skiing is at the end of the beginners' progression, but that doesn't mean you've learnt everything there is to know about skiing – see the short final chapter that follows.

6 LOOKING AHEAD

If you've enjoyed this book and found it useful, please consider giving it a review.

The five chapters preceding this one take you from complete beginner to the end of the beginner's progression. You should now have reached the stage of being able to do basic parallel turns. At this point, I hope you're finding skiing a lot of fun, and you want to do more and get better.

Beyond basic parallel turns, there's more to learn. Advanced skiing is often divided up into these disciplines: carving, short turns, bumps, steep slopes and off piste.

I hope to cover these more advanced techniques in a second book.

Good luck with your skiing!

ABOUT VAL THORENS

Val Thorens is a great ski resort - the highest in Europe, and part of the huge 3 Valleys ski area. I've thoroughly enjoyed my seasons there. The skiing possibilities are extensive, from carving on Tete Ronde to floating on fresh snow down to the Lac du Lou. It's a dynamic resort, always thinking ahead and making things better for visitors. Of course, ski resorts rely on cold weather and snow, and nearly everyone who lives and works in Val Thorens has noticed rapid changes in recent years as the climate heats up. Like all ski resorts, Val Thorens is now facing a big challenge to reduce its own contribution to global heating and to become more sustainable. This will require careful thought and difficult decisions. It may mean less economic activity, not more. I hope Val Thorens will meet the challenge and continue to thrive in the years to come.

Printed in Great Britain
by Amazon

32372127R00050